Education as a Career

Education as a Career

by Arlene Plevin

A joint publication of
American Association for
Counseling and Development
American School
Counselors Association
National Education Association

nea PROFESSIONAL LIBRARY
National Education Association
Washington, D.C.

Library of Congress Cataloging-in-Publication Data

Plevin, Arlene.
    Education as a career / by Arlene Plevin.
        p.   cm.
    ''A joint publication of American Association for Counseling and Development, American School Counselors Association, National Education Association.''
    ISBN 0-8106-1462-6
    1. Teaching—Vocational guidance—United States. I. Title.
LB1775.P59 1988
370'.23' 73—dc19   87-28157
                                                                          CIP

Contents

The Advisory Committee

*Our progress as a nation
can be no swifter than
our progress in
education . . . the
human mind is our
fundamental resource.*

*John F. Kennedy in his
message to Congress on
February 20, 1961*

Introduction

A hundred years ago, a typical school was composed of a single room, desks, a blackboard, and most important of all—a teacher. But just as society itself has grown more complex, so has the educational enterprise. The demands placed upon it are infinitely greater: we expect it to reach not only the educationally able but also those who are developmentally disadvantaged. We expect it to reach a far higher percentage of children and adults than ever before and to be sensitive to the most culturally diverse student population in our history.

Reading, writing, and arithmetic are still the beginning elements of education, but schools are prepared to address much more than subjects when family or psychological problems impinge on students' ability to learn. They must enable students to build self-confidence, to face a future that demands educated individuals who can participate in their own governing.

Teachers are still at the heart of the educational endeavor; however, teachers become more effective as a result of the support provided to them and their students by a host of other professional and skilled workers. Individuals employed as librarians, counselors, nurses, psychologists, purchasing agents, nutritionists, secretaries, and principals are essential to the smooth functioning of schools and colleges. Each in some way promotes the learning process.

Together they make it possible for the nation's schools, colleges, and universities to serve a diverse student population of more than 57 million, ranging in age from two to ninety. The quality of all these educational institutions depends, as it always has, upon the caliber of the people who work in them—their vigor, commitment, and knowledge.

Describing the challenges and rewards of the varied careers in education, this monograph is written to illustrate the numerous options available and to attract capable people to the field. Not only do we explore the many professions that make up the educational enterprise, but we also examine some ways to prepare for a career in education.

Why Education?

*Freedom to learn is
the first necessity of
guaranteeing that
man himself shall be
self-reliant enough to
be free.*

*Franklin D. Roosevelt, in a
speech in New York City on
June 30, 1938*

A nation's principal resource is its people, economist Adam Smith asserted, and the responsibility of educators is to improve that resource. We have made it our nation's mission to encourage all members of society to acquire the basic skills of communication and much, much more. This access to education we consider a right. It reflects our belief that only through education can equality of opportunity be assured, and it recognizes what education contributes to our lives as a people and as a nation.

Many look to education to improve the quality of their daily existence. Mastering a skill, comprehending a concept, and studying a subject is important for personal growth and a feeling of self-worth. Indeed, the intrinsic and extrinsic rewards of education are diverse: there is pleasure in the learning process itself. Education offers the possibility to learn about and understand the world and oneself; its pursuit adds meaning to the individual's life and the life of society.

Certainly there is little debate on education's fundamental value. Our forebears stressed education's importance and Thomas Jefferson recognized this, writing that there is "No other sure foundation...devised for the preservation of freedom and happiness.... [than]...the diffusion of knowledge among the people." In Jefferson's time and ours, education has proved to be vital for a people to participate knowledgeably in their own government. Being a member of a democracy requires the ability to read, write, and exercise judgment. It is paramount to obtain those skills necessary to function successfully in our own society and on the job.

The importance of education is perhaps even greater today. In a changing economic environment, strong basic skills are essential for workers who might need to be retrained or to find new careers. The diverse and often unpredictable job market means that those who are undereducated will be unprepared; they will not be able to take their place in a society that increasingly demands more sophisticated work skills.

Those who have not availed themselves of educational opportunities, perhaps remaining functionally illiterate, will find that only the lowest paying and least desirable jobs are available to them. Many will become marginal to mainstream society and place increasing burdens on various public services and, by extension, on the taxpayers. Enabling everyone to pursue education ensures that they—and the country—will be more prepared for whatever the future brings.

Education: Its Changing Face, Its Continuing Importance

In 1985, over $285 billion was spent on education: it has become the biggest industry in the United States. As state and local legislatures seek to improve their school systems and the quality of their students' experience, it can be assumed that even more funding will be allocated to support the success of this enterprise.

This support is necessary because the very makeup of those who attend public and private schools, community colleges, and universities is changing profoundly. By 1990, one-fourth of the students will be from minorities (in cities such as Los Angeles and Houston, this figure already approaches 50 percent) and half the students will be from single-parent families. One in four will live in poverty.

Large numbers of individuals who desire midcareer changes will turn to the many varieties of adult education programs. In community colleges, universities, career development centers, and vocational/technical training facilities, they will explore retraining in their search for better economic opportunities and greater personal satisfaction.

While these trends indicate that there will be a demand for more bilingual educators and more adult education, they also highlight the importance of a comprehensive education for every person. Each immigrant, each developmentally disadvantaged student, and each adult will have better opportunities to succeed if they receive an education in the basic skills. It must be noted, however, that basic skills for the twenty-first century will be more complex than the three "R's" of decades ago. They will include critical thinking, reasoning, and analytical skills. These skills will enable individuals to achieve their own potential and goals, and to contribute to the growth and productivity of their society.

These are considerations that will affect the educational system and the nature of learning. The nation, in its constant effort to evaluate and improve the educational system, recognizes the changing face of the student population and the resulting challenges. These are challenges that must be met by the field of education. Any number of career options in education provide a forum to affect the quality of individual lives and larger groups of people. With committed individuals, themselves educated and aware, entering the field of education, the goal of educating the many and providing the tools for a promising future can be achieved.

People with skills in administration, management, instruction, organization, guidance, recruitment, fund raising, research, oral and written communication, and caring are sought. There is a need for them and there is a place for them. The educational enterprise offers innumerable possibilities for their commitment, preparation, and talent to be utilized and appreciated.

It is not an easy time to be in education, nor has it ever been. What the field of education provides, however, is a place for people who desire to make a difference either through quiet commitment or energetic enthusiasm. There's a need for people with confidence in their abilities who wish to help others improve their lives.

This opportunity to make a difference is not freely found. Reflecting this special quality, 1981-1982 National Teacher of the Year Jay Sommer stated, "We really are people chosen for a very particular function—to serve in the army that fights ignorance."

Why Choose Education?

*The important thing
is not so much that
every child should be
taught, as that every
child should be given
the wish to learn.*

Sir John Lubbock, 1984

*I*n the morning, out of buses and car pools, pour the reasons why those in secondary and elementary education choose their profession. Excited and energetic, these students tend not to enter the school day quietly. They enter with a bang.

They are Asian, Mexican, Black, and white; they come from Cambodia, Rumania, Guatemala, Ethiopia, Vietnam, and down the street. Their heterogeneity brings new meaning to the term "melting pot," and their numbers swell classes. Reflecting the constantly changing composition of the United States, they arrive with diverse languages and expectations.

They can be exuberant, shy, problematic, gentle, noisy, and fun. Watching them in action, one might simultaneously be exhausted by their energy and stimulated by their differences. They are young learners and the challenge of working with them embraces all the joys and pains that working with any age group in education would entail.

People enter the field of education for innumerable reasons, many because their priority is to help others. They enjoy being around students and they want to further learning. Pursuing a career in education enables them to make a significant difference in individual lives, for few occupations are as challenging as those in the field of education or offer such opportunities to influence others' lives.

Often, attempts to reach a student bring an immediate response, one that is seen in the student's transition from confusion to understanding. Other times, the help given will be acknowledged years later as a former student's achievements are relayed by a parent or sibling. There are satisfactions obtained from these successes, however large or small, that tend to outweigh the profession's detractions.

To many, it is an appealing aspect of education to watch students develop, to know that one can be a part of—indeed, an aid in—that process. Enhancing that experience for many is the opportunity to share information about a favored and well-studied subject. Teaching, for example, allows the enthusiastic sharing of facts and personal experience. In this career and others in education, one's actions have consequences. In such a setting, it is possible to excite a student so that he or she continues to pursue a subject long after the class has ended.

While students are the primary learners in such situations, they are not alone. The questions they ask can inspire educators to reconsider their information, to continue research, and to gain a new perspective. This is one of the dynamic aspects of education—the dialogue where experiences and information are exchanged. Educational professionals are then a part of the learning process. They are taught by their students and they, too, grow and continue developing.

As interactions like these reveal, education is not merely a one-way street where information is dispensed. Through dialogue, recognizing the individual worth of the students, and learning from them, all educational personnel form a partnership. Their partners in learning are all the members of the school family—the students, parents, other support personnel, and their colleagues.

Indeed, if the desire to continually form learning partnerships and increase one's own knowledge is a career criterion, education offers such an opportunity. An important aspect of the education professional's day is to keep current with one's field. The fostering of learning necessitates that a professional stay abreast of relevant developments and be able to communicate them well.

It is true that a number of people who work with students have complained that the opportunity to keep current is not always readily available. They have requested more time for collegial exchange, citing its importance to their professional development. This is an issue that members of the profession, professional associations, and state and local governments are seeking to address. In some school districts, traditional scheduling and traditional "in-service" days are being modified to better meet this need. Other pilot programs are underway, striving to create additional learning occasions for educational personnel and working on solving other problems.

With the beginning of the school year, every member of the educational team starts over again. For many, this new beginning means that lifelong learning and rediscovery is an invigorating part of their lives. Members of the educational team find each year's group of new students exciting and value this ability to start anew. The students themselves can surprise and delight with a unique perspective. To be a partner in their development and to experience their diverse personalities are benefits few professions offer.

Those who prize creativity will find places to express it in education. Tutoring, designing curricula, mediating, motivating, planning, counseling, advising—all of these specialized activities and more, require flexibility and creativity. In an educational setting, both secretaries and superintendents may be called upon to use these talents. As interaction among colleagues, the community, and all educational personnel continue to be encouraged, creativity can flourish.

Insight is another skill that education demands. Students are a challenge. They may give no clue as to what they need, or they may be absolutely blatant about what they require. People who are insightful and like using this skill, will have ample opportunity to do so. Among other things, they can diagnose students' learning, social, and psychological difficulties and do something about them.

Some prefer the opportunity to play a role in organizational or system leadership. Many enjoy the immediate response that comes from direct intervention. For people who enjoy making decisions, examining complex issues, arbitrating, persuading, and negotiating, education offers a variety of supervisory and administrative roles in which these can be used. For those who enjoy positions that are highly visible in the community, the role of superintendent, principal, college president or dean, and others can fulfill that criterion.

Individuals who work in education have formed professional associations to work for the improvement of education. These organizations do much to champion the cause of public education and bring its needs to public attention. They also serve the needs of their members by improving their professional knowledge and practice and enhancing their professional status.

There is increasing public awareness of factors that undercut the satisfactions that come with a career in education. Currently, efforts to improve the status of teachers are underway in many states. Increased opportunities for professional development, improved salaries, increased planning time, and better working conditions are being provided in many states and communities.

At this time, a person does not go into education solely for financial remuneration. Teachers and other education employees tend to be underpaid, receiving a salary that is often less than they could obtain in other fields. This is a serious issue and the financial status of these professionals is likely to improve. Many are seeking to better salaries so that education will attract and keep the kinds of individuals it needs. There are, it is important to add, other essential satisfactions that people in the education profession emphasize while at the same time seeking to increase the limited financial reward.

In all the places of learning—elementary and secondary schools, community colleges, universities, and preschools—are the opportunities to fully use any or all of the humanitarian qualities of caring, teaching, sharing. The more than 57 million students present more opportunities than their numbers to be a part of the learning process and an integral part of someone's memory.

The skills and characteristics necessary for a career in education are special; a commitment to it marks the choice to affect the future. One professional, switching from program analyst to teaching math and coordinating computers at a junior high school explained, "I wanted to do meaningful work."

PART III

Options in Education

*The secret of
education lies in
respecting the pupil.*

Ralph Waldo Emerson

S chools and universities employ nearly six million people who work in instructional, administrative, supervisory, and other capacities. The new group of young children in the current "baby boomlet" and the usual job turnover among education employees in high schools, colleges, and universities create a continuous need for capable individuals. And as schools continue striving to reach a changing population, they will restructure, creating even more career opportunities in education.

On the Front Line: Teaching

Teaching is one of the most challenging, interesting, and influential of careers. It is also one of the most underpaid, underrated, and demanding. Whatever other workers are employed to enhance the instructional process, teachers are its heart.

Teaching provides an immediacy and intensity that is rare in many jobs today; often teachers can see changes in their students as they grow in knowledge and understanding.

Teaching requires knowledge of subject matter, an ability to impart information clearly, and an understanding of how children and adults learn. It also requires patience, sensitivity, and tenacity as students learn at different speeds, respond to different kinds of presentations, and have different motivational needs. A teacher must know not only how to instruct, but also how to guide and encourage a heterogeneous group of students with various levels of skill. And a teacher must know how to balance the needs of the individual students with those of the class as a whole.

The techniques teachers use to impart information and encourage learning are varied: they include the formal ones of lecture, demonstration, discussion, question and answer, and extend to the use of drama and humor. For many teachers, this performance aspect is an appealing part of their career. Whatever aspect of teaching satisfies the most, there is no doubt that teaching is an art. Many techniques are employed by teachers, and all of them illustrate the complex nature of successful teaching.

Many teachers maintain it is important to like sharing your knowledge. And it is this pleasure in sharing that puts teachers in a position to receive the affection and respect of students. For many students, teachers become role models. Valuing their expertise and responsiveness, students might seek their advice and plan on becoming teachers themselves. Indeed, having others follow your example is a "heady" reward. It is also because teachers can be powerful examples, inspiring their students to choose the path they have chosen, that people representing more and more cultures are needed to enter the teaching profession to share their skills and background. A diverse faculty that accurately represents the makeup of society allows all students to have access to the educational team they deserve.

Teaching as a profession is changing. The isolation and lack of contact with each other that many teachers have noted in past years is being addressed. Task forces and committees, commissioned by federal, state, and local governments, have recognized the urgency of implementing reforms that will improve teachers' working conditions and the learning process. Improved financial rewards, and increased opportunities to interact with colleagues and to have a voice in instructional decisions are some of the changes being discussed and implemented.

Early Childhood Education

With increasing numbers of women joining the workforce, more people who specialize in the care of young children will be needed. People who enjoy taking care of young children and offering early learning activities may find employment in day care centers or preschool centers. Supervisors of these centers are specialists in early childhood education and can structure learning opportunities in the daily environment.

Preschool centers' clients are children from ages three to five who need care and attention during their parents' working hours. Because of increasing numbers of two-career families and working single parents, there is a corresponding demand for quality care in this area. Many centers, recognizing the workday schedule, have hours on a par with those of their children's parents.

Teachers in preschool centers focus on the development of the children, introducing new experiences, encouraging language and social skills, and, in general, preparing them for school. Social workers, psychologists, nutritionists, nurses, clerks, teacher aides, audiologists, counselors, playground supervisors—in short, many of the same helping personnel who support learning at the elementary, secondary, and higher education level—are needed. They all help to introduce children to learning and get them off to a good start.

Elementary and Secondary Instructional Staff

At the elementary school level, one teacher is usually responsible for most of the subject areas: reading, arithmetic, social studies, basic science, and so on. He or she typically works with the same class on a daily basis although other teachers in specialized subjects may visit to enrich the regular class work. This daily interaction with the same group of students permits the teacher to recognize individual needs of students and to structure the class accordingly. For any teacher, however, it is a challenge to balance the needs of the individual with those of the class.

There are special rewards in teaching children: the excitement of seeing them encounter certain concepts for the first time, their humor and often surprising precociousness, their sensitivity to the teacher's demands, their zest and energy. Experienced teachers often comment on the trust their students place in them. Many enjoy teaching for the opportunity it affords to nurture the rapid intellectual and emotional growth that occurs in elementary school-age students. These students can sometimes be exhausting—but they are also a great deal of fun and offer immeasurable satisfactions.

At the high school and junior high school level, teachers instruct students in one or two subjects that are in their area of expertise. English and language arts, foreign languages, history and social studies, industrial arts, mathematics, physical education and health, home economics, science, vocational subjects, art, and music are some of the areas in which a secondary school teacher may specialize.

By working with older students at the junior high school and high school level, these professionals will see students begin to enter the adult world and they will continue the progression their students have begun in elementary school toward developing critical thinking, writing proficiency, and other complex skills. Many will help their students consider and explore career goals and options.

Whatever the age of the students, both elementary and secondary level teachers must develop methods appropriate to the group with which they work and to the various levels of ability within a class. Right now, teachers should be prepared to do some of the tasks that usually are associated with a job in a school, whether supervising lunchrooms or doing the necessary paperwork that goes along with a teaching position. While efforts are being made to reduce noninstructional activities and the use of teacher aides sometimes reduces the burden of these noninstructional duties, they are an aspect of most teachers' working day.

College, University, and Community College Instructional Staff

Instructional staff in these levels of higher education work primarily with adult students and have varying responsibilities. All strive to further their students' body of knowledge and to help them achieve their goals. They may be professors, instructors, deans, department heads, or adjunct faculty. At this level, there are opportunities to exercise professional judgment in coursework. More often than not, a certain amount of research or scholarship is expected. For all of these instructional personnel, their positions are governed by the goals of their students, whether they are attending a community college, a four-year college, or a university.

Students who attend community college may wish to prepare for a specific job, transfer to a four-year institution, increase their job training, or pursue additional education while they work at a full-time job. At the same time, many of these students are older, are returning to school after a long absence, and are highly committed to learning.

The community college staff enables all of these students' goals. At the community college, teaching is stressed while research tends to be deemphasized. In some respects, community colleges are more connected with the local community, drawing many of their students from the immediate area. Instructional faculty tend to teach four to six classes.

At the four-year college, instructional personnel are expected to continually research their discipline and to stay current with developments in their field. Their commitment to research is often measured by their productivity; many publish books and present papers. Their teaching load tends to be less than that of the community college staff as it is believed that doing research is important in order to remain in the forefront of their field.

Instructional personnel at the community college, college, and university level have usually completed a doctorate degree. Involving four years of undergraduate study and four to seven years of graduate study, plus the writing of a dissertation, these degrees imply in-depth research and study of one or more areas. Tenure, or a continuing position with a university or community college, can occur after three to seven years, when a faculty member has been evaluated as successful, usually in a process involving his or her peers.

Specialties: Changing and Emerging Roles in Teaching

Vocational, Technical, and Adult Education Teachers

Across the country, there are as many different types of vocational, technical, and adult education programs as there are school districts. These programs offer students the opportunity to develop valuable skills, try out various career options, and, in general, continue the pursuit of lifelong learning.

Many vocational programs are located within high schools, giving attending students a chance to explore diverse interests. These programs, which range from automobile repair to painting, from woodworking to computers, from construction to printing to culinary arts, are presented in a setting that emphasizes hands-on learning. Similar programs are frequently offered to adult students on a noncredit basis.

At the high school level and at community colleges, these courses not only give students experience but are part of larger programs that result in diplomas, certificates or associate of arts degrees. Some content areas are distributive education, health occupations, home economics, office work, technical occupations, and trade and industrial occupations. These programs are useful both for students who do not wish to pursue a college degree and for those who desire further education for career advancement or personal enrichment.

Many districts have adult education centers, career development centers, and apprenticeship schools that have similar goals but different methods. One major purpose is adult basic education leading to achievement of an alternative high school credential such as the General Educational Development Diploma or the External High School Diploma. Some centers and schools offer evening classes and instruction. Whatever academic competencies and work-related skills and techniques are considered relevant to the profession sought are practiced in these centers. Not all of the courses prepare one for a career; many of them are considered enrichment courses, offering working adults the time to improve skills and learn new ones that are not necessarily job-related. Many adults take courses outside of their area of expertise to learn about new subjects and just to continue the important process of learning. These programs are often intergenerational: high school students may attend part time, sharing classrooms with older adults.

Vocational and adult education programs may be located in high schools, specialized vocational high schools, community colleges, four-year colleges, universities, and state and federal training programs.

Teachers in these programs may be part time or full time. They offer courses that enable students to build confidence and skills by directly meeting their education and employment needs. Teachers in vocational education have usually specialized in a particular field such as fashion merchandising, photography, or journalism. Teachers in adult education may have a graduate degree in adult education or may have a degree in their specific field.

Enabling students of all ages to understand what they might contribute to the world of work and to their own personal growth is a rewarding opportunity. Teaching people who are self-motivated and bring their life experiences to the classroom is an incentive for teachers in these fields.

Special Education Teachers

Special education teachers work with emotionally disturbed, developmentally disabled, and physically disabled students. Their classes tend to be small in order for them to give their students the attention, instruction, and caring they need. For many students enrolled in special education classes, their teacher can make the difference between their learning and succeeding or being unable to reach their potential.

Special education teachers need patience and strong coping skills. Achievements in special education classes may be small by some standards but large when the students' initial obstacles are taken into account. For some special education teachers, their reward is in their special students' pleasure over new competencies and the parents' gratitude for this growth.

Bilingual Teachers

With the coming decades promising even greater increases in minority students, the skills of bilingual teachers are quite important to a school system. Fluent in English and any number of other languages—Spanish, Mandarin, Russian, Vietnamese, Portugese, French, and Native American languages—bilingual teachers conduct classes, staff reading and writing labs, and act as interpreters for the vast numbers of non-English proficient students who have entered and will enter the school system.

The purpose of bilingual education is to use a student's native language as a bridge to the learning of English while developing skill in other academic areas. Bilingual teachers work with students to achieve this goal so that English becomes their second language. Because bilingual teachers may sometimes be the only professionals capable of understanding a student's native tongue, they are often called on to translate and help the student understand responsibilities and options. Once the bilingual teacher has successfully instructed students, they will then be more ready to function well in the school and society, communicating with peers and school personnel.

Supporting the Learner: Helping Professions in the Schools

Counselor, social worker, psychologist, speech therapist, hearing therapist, audiologist, psychometrist—these careers are some that come under the auspices of student personnel services or student development. They reflect education's commitment to provide support for the total human growth of the student.

Librarians and Media Specialists

Reflecting the growing amount of information and how it is processed, librarians and media specialists work with all sorts of data. The world of books, computers, microfiche, videotapes, records, slides, and other ways of storing images and information is the domain of these specialists. Some libraries are called resource centers, but whatever the title, their personnel are crucial to students' intellectual development. For those who enjoy the sharing of words and the retrieval of information, the career of school librarian, media specialist, or library aide is one to consider.

Librarians instruct students so that they can confidently use all of the resources in the resource center. Librarians stay current on publications relevant to the age and level of the students they serve, order books, catalogue material, and organize all printed material. In some school systems, they may organize and operate the audiovisual center. Many teach classes on effective use of the library. With the boom in information, librarians are often expected to be able to access other libraries through the computer.

Media specialists, and often librarians, may be responsible

for film storage, equipment management and use, and for instructing students so that they can use all equipment correctly. Media specialists might be experts in one area such as young adult films, and may make recommendations to teachers searching for relevant material.

Counselors

Counselors' expertise is in psychological development, and they are familiar with educational policy and community resources. In every school setting, they work with students to enable them to develop fully and to realize their intellectual, emotional, and social promise. Counselors assist with problem solving by offering students information and encouragement.

Much of what counselors do is oriented toward anticipating and preventing problems in the student and the school. They cooperate with other members of the school staff to identify problems early. Students having difficulty might be identified and referred to the counselor by any member of the educational team who has observed a need for guidance. Aware of relevant resources inside and outside the school, the counselor will put students in contact with helping agencies or, if appropriate, work with those students and their families directly. Recognizing that a student distracted by personal problems cannot possibly learn effectively, the counselor will confer confidentially with that student. A counselor's insight and ability to listen and guide will be utilized.

To effectively counsel the many students who seek their aid, counselors are creative and flexible. They develop programs to help students discuss societal problems such as teenage pregnancy, drug abuse, alcoholism, and child abuse. Meeting individually with students, sometimes conferring with both parents and students, is another part of a counselor's day.

Counselors also stay current with developments in career and educational options so that they may best counsel their students. Understanding new ways of testing aptitude for various careers is another aspect of the counselors' responsibility since they help students explore career options. From kindergarten through college, counselors work with students to help them assess their abilities and interests, set life and career goals, and make plans to achieve them.

Elementary school counselors use a developmental approach to counseling and they help students develop a sense of self-worth.

Secondary and postsecondary school counselors continue this process and help students establish a career direction by providing relevant and helpful material and offering tests that can aid in educational planning and career assessment.

Working with other knowledgeable student personnel, counselors assist in identifying problems of students, help organize in-service programs for members of the staff, implement career programs, provide information on social services, and plan strategies to deal effectively with any number of problems faced by students. They enable students to develop self-awareness and self-confidence and work with them to remove obstacles to learning—and growth. For all aspects of this process, a thorough knowledge of psychological development is essential.

School Social Workers

Social workers focus on people and the environment; in the school setting, their contribution is often to help children and families deal with difficult family problems that might interfere with a child's ability to learn. Familiar with educational policy and legislation, they are knowledgeable about both the school system and community resources.

It is unusual for the school social worker to be located in one school. For the most part, they are responsible for several schools or for an entire school district and may travel from school to school to fulfill the responsibilities of the position. The school social worker functions as a liaison with a student's teacher and family, and with outside organizations such as state or local agencies that may be involved in funding or legal action, and with special schools or programs where a student may receive services. Often they work in tandem with school counselors, both professionals striving to provide the maximum support to the student.

Social workers may provide assessment of the student in the context of his/her family and the classroom, and assist in the development of a plan of action for helping the student, whether for special tutoring, counseling, different placement in the same school, or transfer to another educational setting. Sometimes the social worker is called upon to make recommendations to parents about the kinds of assistance they should obtain if the student is to be helped.

The social worker may have to confront some of the more difficult problems in our society such as families in great internal conflict, child abuse or neglect, physical or mental illness in the child or parents, alcoholism, teenage pregnancy, or a host of other problems. The school social worker's job is to find solutions that will work for the student, for his or her family, and for the school system. Social workers must be knowledgeable about the resources available for helping a student and adept at dealing with students and families in distress.

Psychometrists and School Psychologists

Psychometrists and school psychologists enable schools to more effectively diagnose and treat students' difficulties. A psychometrist's specialty is administering, scoring, and interpreting tests. These tests are tools that help assess intelligence, aptitude, and achievement and can be useful for diagnosing what is presenting problems for students. These tests also help to determine students' strengths and weaknesses.

In the school setting, psychologists are part of the team that assists students in a variety of ways. They interpret diagnostic tests, developing plans to help students. By providing individual and group therapy for students, they contribute to the efforts of teachers, social workers, and counselors. As part of the team supporting learners, they assist in eliminating whatever prevents a student from becoming psychologically healthy and participating fully in school.

School Health Services

School nurses, dental hygienists, speech and hearing therapists, and audiologists—these professionals and others concern themselves with the physical health of the student. They may be part of a larger department, such as a university health center, or work by themselves. They focus on prevention of illness and disability and detection and correction of health problems. Many times, they organize schoolwide programs designed to inform students of preventive health care. Alert to ailments that might prevent learning and hamper the growth of the individual, they may recommend outside treatment or directly assist the student.

In preschool, elementary, and secondary schools, the school nurse may be the primary giver of medical care. She or he may sponsor instructional programs to provide a school's staff and students with up-to-date health information and will do physical assessments of students. Usually, the school nurse is the first on the scene in medical emergencies. Consequently, the school nurse often evaluates all injuries occurring on the school's premises, treating and referring them when appropriate. Depending on the age of a school's students, a school nurse will provide care appropriate to the illnesses and injuries that are most likely to occur. Aware of elementary, secondary, or college students' specialized needs, a school nurse is an integral part of the educational team that strives to support the student in all aspects.

Speech and hearing therapists work with students with diagnosed difficulties. A student with a stutter may use a speech therapist's expertise in conquering this communication impairment. A hearing therapist will diagnose hearing problems and work with students so that they may function to the best of their ability. Both therapists usually work with individual students, helping them achieve their goals.

The dental hygienist instructs students on how to prevent dental problems, diagnoses some dental problems, and refers students to the appropriate source of help. In some schools, a dental hygienist might be the only professional who oversees this aspect of students' health care.

Dieticians

The dietician is trained in nutrition and skilled in supervising the preparation of large quantities of food. Usually, hundreds of people depend on the school's cafeteria so the dietician must constantly research ways to vary the selection of food and present it appealingly. Responsibility for the cafeteria's food budget is another domain of the dietician; he or she must be aware of economical ways of buying food. In some schools, a dietician may prepare food in addition to planning meals.

Administration and Management

The goal of principals, superintendents, and college and university administrators is to support student achievement. This is accomplished through effective leadership, attention to quality functioning of schools, responsiveness to staff and students' needs, and an understanding of what nurtures learning.

Superintendents are concerned with several schools or an entire school district. A background in teaching enhances their ability to understand the teaching and learning process and the factors that affect them. For the most part, the close relationship that teachers have with students is usually not available to superintendents. In their supervisory capacity, they rarely have an opportunity to be a part of the day-to-day business of a school. Their position can give them the satisfaction obtained from helping the learning progress by effectively managing the school facilities, personnel, and operations. Like all other educational personnel, they are problem solvers.

In their administrative capacity, they must understand the complexities of school district finances. Implementing the current budget and planning for the future are part of their responsibilities. They must plan the budget in advance, foreseeing what programs may require additional funding, for example, and planning for those needs.

Typically, superintendents will coordinate all of a district's resources and represent their district to the Board of Education. They must be effective managers of people, capable of motivating them toward a common end.

Principals usually serve as administrator for one or more schools and have more direct and frequent contact with teachers, counselors and support personnel. They work with curriculum specialists and teachers, counselors and other personnel, organizing meetings and helping to determine schoolwide goals. Through their efforts to improve the climate in which learning takes place, they usually get to know their school's students.

As a key liaison between the school and community, the principal is actively involved with community relations. He or she is likely to be involved with Parent-Teacher Associations (PTAs) and other groups of citizens interested in the schools.

Principals set standards of behavior for students and ensure that the school environment functions smoothly to promote learning. Students may be referred to them and their assistants since part of their job is to deal effectively with those individuals who may be disrupting the school's environment. The final responsibility for the school rests with them. It is important that they understand the nature of teaching and every other position in the education profession so that they can fully support all personnel.

A college or university president usually is qualified in a number of ways to enable him or her to be appointed or elected to the position. In some instances, college presidents may be experienced professors who are well-known and well-respected academicians. Occasionally, individuals from the private sector may be asked to assume this role.

This position demands negotiating, administrative, budgeting, and fund-raising skills. As the representative of a college or university, the president must work with diverse factions who often disagree. Frequently, college or university presidents travel to confer with other leaders in the education field and to represent their school.

At a community college, a president's responsibilities may be more closely tied to direct administration of the school. He or she may be called upon to do public relations for the community college and to lobby the state legislature for funding.

Deans, in charge of a department of a four-year college or university's school, are usually specialists in a particular discipline. A school's Dean of Education, for example, is most likely an individual with teaching and administrative experience. He or she administers a program, looking out for its interests, and advises and supports the program's faculty. Decisions on what direction the curriculum will take, who will be hired, and a department or school's budget are likely to be under a dean's jurisdiction.

Often positions requiring administrative and people-management skills may be found in some areas of university, community college, and four-year college student services. Student union manager, head of student activities, special events coordinator, and ombudsman are some opportunities in student services.

Support Personnel

Integral to the functioning of any school or college are support personnel whose expertise enables other members of the education system to work more effectively. Library and teacher aides, lab technicians, teacher assistants, secretaries, clerical assistants, payroll assistants, custodians, groundskeepers, food service personnel, volunteer coordinators, supply personnel, admissions personnel, recruiters, health center workers, residence hall advisors, security and alumni association personnel are among the many whose skills are needed on a daily basis in schools and colleges.

Library aides assist librarians, extending the librarian's ability to give personal attention to students. Checking out books and recommending resources to students and faculty are services they provide. They may help teachers assemble a collection of books suitable for an upcoming class or assist counselors and social workers in presenting exhibits exploring social problems.

Helping the teacher in everything from arranging materials to giving the students additional personal attention is part of a teacher aide's job description. The teacher aide enables the teacher to be more effective by freeing him or her from time-consuming, noninstructional responsibilities. Teacher aides may take attendance, operate audiovisual equipment, supervise students' recreation time, and work with students in learning activities.

Secretarial and clerical support is necessary for the efficient functioning of any profession and education is no exception. Keeping track of crucial school records, handling phone calls, and informing education personnel about relevant matters is part of their contribution. There is interaction with students of all ages and secretaries may be called upon to help them with paperwork or in contacting parents.

Custodians, groundskeepers, and members of the maintenance staff keep the school environment clean and safe so that the school's facilities are usable at all times. Food service personnel prepare and serve food for all of a school's staff and students.

Schools often attract individuals who enjoy working in such an environment and who may volunteer their time and assistance without pay. The volunteer coordinator places these people in positions where their skills can best be used.

Personnel Unique to Higher Education

Admissions personnel are usually located at the university, four-year college, or community college. Private schools may also employ these personnel. Admissions personnel evaluate prospective students, considering who would prosper at their particular institution. In many instances, they are housed in the registrar's office where recruiters are traditionally placed.

In some respects, recruiters are a school's advance scouts. Eager to attract qualified students and maintain the size of a university's or college's student body, they may travel extensively. To appeal to prospective students, recruiters may present slide shows, sponsor social gatherings, and, in general, represent their school. Often, recruiters are graduates of the institution they represent and therefore are in a unique position to provide information about their school's virtues.

Without knowledge of financing alternatives, many capable students would have to delay advanced education or perhaps forego it entirely. The financial aid specialist at a college or university is an expert in the types of financial aid available, where to apply for aid, who is eligible, and in what combination scholarships and grants can be used. An interest in making education possible for others, a willingness to constantly update one's storehouse of information, and an ability to match students with the best sources of aid are vital components of the financial aid specialist's job.

Living on the school's campus, residence hall advisors interact daily with students. While their responsibility may be to ensure that the dormitory or student dwellings function smoothly, they are often the first person a troubled student will approach. As such, residence hall advisors enjoy warm and open relationships with many students. Residence hall advisors may be upperclass or graduate students who receive free room and board in exchange for their services or they may be nonstudents, hired to live on-campus.

Other support positions include copy center personnel, building maintenance personnel, bus drivers, transportation specialists, mail department personnel, and purchasing agents.

In Summary

Many jobs in our economy are remote from the people, products, or processes affected. By contrast, careers available in education offer a unique kind of immediacy, intensity, and intimacy. There is a need in this growing field for talented and committed people with a wide range of skills. Teaching, counseling, nurturing, instructing, sharing, growing—verbs of doing—describe the nature of a career in education, regardless of the age of the learner with whom one is involved.

Counselor, principal, tutor, vocational-education teacher, dental hygienist, transportation specialist, community relations aide, financial aid specialist, audiologist, ombudsman—this list of educational positions just begins to describe the many possibilities for employment. For people who delight in being around learners, the possibilities are nearly endless.

In the Appendix following Part Five, a listing of careers can be found. Seek out someone in that position for first-hand information. Volunteering to work with that professional is perhaps the best method for researching the position. You will discover what the five million people currently employed in the field of education know: there are difficulties and rewards, delights and frustrations, and there is a satisfying future in working with the ongoing process of learning and in contributing to a field important to our country's future.

Preparing for a Career in Education

The result of the educative process is capacity for further education.

John Dewey

*I*n another century, preparing for a career in education meant studying the basics at a normal school, one of the first teacher training institutes. Established in the mid-1800s, they were typically attended by young women. In these institutions, prospective instructors focused on reading, writing, arithmetic and geography, recognizing that broad knowledge of these subjects would be essential to pass on to their students. There were few choices in education at this time and the normal school's emphasis on the teacher reflected this reality.

Today, preparation is more diverse and rigorous. Involvement in education may be through a variety of positions, and there is no longer one school that specializes in preparing educational personnel for a single role. Because there are many routes to a career in education and a myriad of choices, selecting the best school for your goals means carefully investigating what prospective schools do offer.

One of your considerations may be geographical. Then once you have decided in what region you would like to pursue your studies, examine numerous school catalogues, talk to admissions counselors and professors to gain a clear understanding of what courses are offered and how your needs could be met. Large universities with an undergraduate school of education are one possibility. In addition to the required education courses, these universities will have a variety of liberal arts courses, which many educators feel is an essential part of a student's foundation.

Another option is to enroll in a liberal arts college and study a specific area. After receiving a bachelor's degree in that area of concentration, pursue a master of arts in education (M.Ed.) in a graduate program. Actual experience in a classroom is one of the trademarks of most M.Ed. degrees, which usually include classes in educational philosophy and teaching methodology.

Enrolling in a community or junior college also offers the opportunity for experience in the field as you prepare to enter it. Two years of preparation toward a bachelor's degree in an area of interest is possible, and the community setting permits volunteering for relevant activities or working with professionals who are knowledgeable about your career interests.

Knowing the position you would like to assume in education will, of course, enable you to rigorously examine schools' programs for classes that support that ambition. If you are less certain but recognize, for example, that you would like to work in some capacity with young learners, a school whose strengths are in elementary education may be appropriate. Whichever institution you choose should be accredited by both the recognized regional and national accrediting bodies.

Regardless of your degree of certainty about which position you want, one important determinant should be whether the school offers experience in a practicum or internship setting. Supervised experience prior to a full-time position as a member of the instructional staff is critically important.

In addition to discovering an aptitude (or lack of) for teaching, counseling, or administration, practicums or practice situations allow you to perfect your techniques and learn from experienced personnel.

They also provide opportunities to immerse yourself in the field and find out what is happening at that moment. A more informed evaluation of the various types of educational situations that exist is then possible.

Working in camps, volunteering for civic and community organizations or local agencies, or assisting in a school's office, for example, may further your preparation. These activities provide experience that can be helpful in making a decision as to which aspect of education you would like to pursue and which age group of students you prefer.

In addition to an internship experience and in-depth study of your area of concentration, a broad variety of courses will enhance your preparation. One seeking to teach at the elementary level may focus on several subjects as an undergraduate and take courses leading to certification, obtaining a bachelor's degree in elementary education. Some schools offer prospective secondary school teachers a bachelor's degree in arts and sciences, which includes twelve hours of education courses and student teaching and results in certification. However, some entry-level positions require graduate study.

A variety of options are possible at the graduate level. For students with an undergraduate degree or those with graduate coursework in something other than the study and practice of teaching, some departments of education offer teaching certification programs. In addition to student teaching experience, these programs will likely include courses in curriculum development, methodology, and education's social and philosophical history. Courses in a program leading to teacher certification may involve fieldwork, such as observing at a school, so that students can have additional experience in a school environment.

In addition to a thorough knowledge of a subject and an understanding of the psychology of learning and development, some states may demand graduate study of teaching methods or undergraduate courses in educational philosophy may be mandated. Some states require that prospective teachers take exams such as the National Teachers Exam that prove they meet certain standards. In other areas of education, states mandate that other educational personnel take exams as well. Again, relevant information detailing what requirements are appropriate for the region of your choice can be found in the education department of universities, four-year colleges, community colleges, and state education departments.

It is important to recognize that in teaching, counseling, and other career areas in education, the criteria for certification or licensure will differ from state to state. As this is written, many states are reviewing and changing their requirements for certification and more changes are certain to occur. Therefore, planning for a career in any kind of school setting necessitates contacting the certification office in each state for the most current and detailed information.

Preparing to be a counselor, school social worker, or psychologist requires the detailed study of psychology and human development because these positions are rooted in the behavioral sciences. These positions require a master's degree from an accredited institution and often require teaching experience.

Most schools, consider only individuals with a teaching background for positions in administration. Graduate study in educational administration is also expected to be part of the preparation of a principal, assistant principal, or superintendent.

Some colleges and universities, seeking the expertise of professionals such as lawyers or writers, may hire them to teach part time, calling them lecturers, adjunct faculty, or instructors. These individuals have usually worked professionally in their specialty and bring years of experience in their field to the college classroom. Community colleges, colleges, universities, career and vocational education centers often use these people as part-time instructors. While these positions may not require teaching credentials, rarely do they become full time.

From working in a community college to teaching at an elementary school, preparing for a career in education means evaluating your talents and considering what program would best serve your needs and enhance your skills. While the next section will discuss which settings suggest the greatest possibility for employment, pursue those subjects that excite you. And prepare for a challenging career.

Future Staffing Needs

Currently, our nation is comprised of nearly sixteen thousand school districts, two million teachers, and thirty-nine million students. By the year 1995, these numbers will change as our population grows slowly from 237 million to 260 million. Education and other professions will be affected by this increase and shaped by numerous changes in the composition of our population, the continuing influence of technology, and the changing nature of work.

Many of those forces that affect education will continue to do so as others emerge. New students will enter the school system while some graduate and others drop out. A sizable and increasing number of refugees and immigrants will continue to seek educational opportunities. Some education personnel will accept positions outside of education, retire, or switch to part-time status. Prospective college students may pursue their bachelor's degree or delay it according to the amount of funding available. The demographics of urban centers will change as some residents choose to relocate to rural areas or warmer climates. And a rapidly increasing number of adults, envisioning a change in their career or seeking personal and professional advancement, will return to career centers, community colleges, and vocational schools to continue their growth.

While we know the preceding to be true, every aspect of the future cannot be predicted. The future can be planned for, however. Student enrollment is the key determinant in the demand for administrators, support personnel, and instructional personnel, and there are as many anticipated as unforeseen forces that influence and shape the educational enterprise. Knowing there will be a slight increase in certain age groups and a decrease in others does not make it possible to predict exactly the amount of educational personnel that will be needed. It is possible, however, to point out areas of probable need. And it is possible to suggest geographical areas where people with certain skills and education are likely to be employed.

The nation's birth rate provides some clues. Throughout the mid-1990s, as the age of the population shifts, there will be an increase in the number of children under thirteen and in the number of adults over sixty-five and between the ages of twenty-five to fifty-five. Reflecting the growth in minorities nationwide, the schools will have an increasingly more diverse population. More and more children in the school system will be poor, and many will be from single-parent families. All of this suggests there will be a greater need for minority teachers, basic education personnel, and personnel who work with adults returning to school. It is also important that education personnel understand their students' varied backgrounds.

Based on the U.S. Bureau of the Census statistics, the number of elementary school pupils will rise slightly by the mid-1990s, with projected increases running from 0.5 to 1.4 percent. The number of secondary school pupils has declined slightly in the last five years and will continue to do so until 1991, when the number of secondary school students will increase again.

According to these and other indicators, there are more openings in elementary education and this will continue to be true for many years. Projections by the U.S. Department of Labor's Bureau of Labor Statistics place kindergarten teachers, with a percent change of 29.9, as among one of the top twenty-five fastest-growing occupations for 1984 through 1995. It is estimated that over 432,000 new kindergarten teachers will be needed by 1995.

Teaching opportunities at the postsecondary level are not as plentiful. While experts differ and some point to minutely increased opportunities for young scholars, most agree that chances of employment as a professor, especially in the humanities, are limited. After the 1990s, as more instructional personnel at the college, university, and community college level retire, there may be more opportunities at those levels.

Currently, there are fairly severe teacher shortages in such subject areas as mathematics, chemistry, physics, and computer programming. Other less severe shortages exist in bilingual education, special education, and general science. These shortages are expected to continue for the next ten years.

Years ago, a mass movement of people from the Northeast and Midwest regions to states considered to be in the "Sunbelt" was predicted. While millions have moved to Florida, California, Texas, and Georgia, giving those states the greatest gains in population from 1980–1985, there has not been the massive drain of people from the northern states as originally suggested. Instead, new figures point to the Northeast as maintaining its population with modest increases. States demonstrating the most growth probably will be North Carolina, Florida, Texas, and California. Other states, most notably in the East North Central region—including Illinois, Michigan, Ohio, and Wisconsin—may experience a loss of population. According to the Bureau of the Census, the fastest growing region of the country will be the West. The Bureau of the Census also projects that the West and the South will have 60 percent of the population by the year 2000. What this suggests is that elementary school personnel in those states will be in the most demand while in other areas there will be more competition for fewer positions.

Regardless of geographical considerations, adult and continuing education in its many manifestations is one of the rapidly growing areas in education. By 1993, there will be more people over the age of thirty in college than under the age of twenty-one. This "graying" of the student population reflects not only the demographic truth that the number of adults is increasing, but that learning is a lifelong process. Adults are returning to school to retrain, to rethink their career goals, and to enjoy mastering new subjects and skills. There will be many opportunities to work with corporations, community colleges, and career centers as adults continue their education. Some of these positions will be part time, however.

Overall, the need for support personnel is tied to the birth rate. In some communities, as enrollments decline, schools may consolidate and staff cutbacks are likely. While the need for certain types of personnel in certain regions of the nation will not be high, the increasing nationwide recognition of education's importance and a tangible commitment to its improvement suggests that there will be support and encouragement for the best and the brightest to enter this field. The changing face of the student population and the need for all to have basic skills for the twenty-first century require skilled, committed, and knowledgeable people in all levels of the educational enterprise. It is indeed a time of change, of opportunity. Because of the public's increasing commitment to education, there is support for leadership in education and for innovations that will benefit both students and the vast team of educational personnel.

PART V

Summing Up

I am an educator! The future of the world is in my classroom. I have the opportunity to inspire my students to dream great dreams, and to help them gain the will, the skill, and the knowledge they need to turn their dreams into realities.

Mary Hatwood Futrell,
President,
National Education
Association

*T*he scale in which educational enterprises are carried out in the nation is inspiring. Millions of educational personnel rally around and support the student, the center of all educational activity. Nearly sixteen thousand school districts discuss how to improve their handling of problems, how best to deliver a thorough and challenging education to their charges. They plan and argue, research and prioritize. They are, in all their exciting and maddening diversity, representative of the trials and challenges facing the nation's entire educational system.

The field of education has much to do in the next twenty years if it is to continue to reach and challenge students and continue to strive to affect all its members. And its personnel—teachers, librarians, counselors, secretaries, principals, students, and all the other team members—have much to do as well.

But while much remains to be done, much is being accomplished. Responsive, caring people concerned with supporting the learner are stepping in and seeking a profession whose rewards are legendary. It is a profession that actively discusses its difficulties and the changes that must be made. That parents, students, legislators, governors, and governmental leaders focus on what has been accomplished and what remains to be done is a measure of education's fundamental importance.

To pursue a career in any of the options available in education is to join the ranks of committed individuals. To choose education means recognizing the potential for obstacles and difficulties. But this choice is also made recognizing you can contribute your skills to a profession known for its caring for students, its nurturing of the human spirit.

Appendix A:
Suggested Resources

The following is a brief listing of some organizations, associations, and departments that will have additional information on specific careers in education to aid your decision making. Consult your school's counselor as well for additional information and suggestions.

American Alliance for Health,
   Physical Education,
   Recreation, and Dance
1900 Association Drive
Reston, VA 22091

American Association for Adult
   and Continuing Education
1201 16th Street, N.W.
Washington, D.C. 20036

American Association for Colleges
   of Teacher Education
One Dupont Circle, N.W.
Suite 610
Washington, D.C. 20036

American Association for
   Counseling and Development
5999 Stevenson Avenue
Alexandria, VA 22304

American Association for Higher
   Education
One Dupont Circle, N.W.
Washington, D.C. 20036

**American Association of School
   Administrators**
1801 North Moore Street
Arlington, VA 22209

**American Association of State
   Colleges and Universities**
One Dupont Circle, N.W.
Washington, D.C. 20036

**American School Counselors
   Association**
5999 Stevenson Avenue
Alexandria, VA 22304

American Vocational Association
2020 North 14th Street
Arlington, VA 22201

**Association for Supervision
   and Curriculum Development**
125 North West Street
Alexandria, VA 22314

Association of Teacher Educators
1900 Association Drive
Reston, VA 22091

Council for Exceptional Children
1920 Association Drive
Reston, VA 22091

**Music Educators National
   Conference**
1902 Association Drive
Reston, VA 22091

National Art Education Association
1916 Association Drive
Reston, VA 22091

**National Association of Elementary
School Principals**
1615 Duke Street
Alexandria, VA 22314

**National Association of Secondary
School Principals**
1904 Association Drive
Reston, VA 22091

**National Association of Social
Workers**
7981 Eastern Avenue
Silver Spring, MD 20910

**National Career Development
Association**
5999 Stevenson Avenue
Alexandria, VA 22304

**National Council for
the Social Studies**
3501 Newark Street, N.W.
Washington, D.C. 20016

**National Council of Teachers
of English**
1111 Kenyon Road
Urbana, IL 61801

**National Council of Teachers
of Mathematics**
1906 Association Drive
Reston, VA 22091

National Education Association
1201 16th Street, N.W.
Washington, D.C. 20036

**National Parent-Teacher
 Association**
700 North Rush Street
Chicago, IL 60611

**National School Boards
 Association**
1680 Duke Street
Alexandria, VA 22314

**National Science Teachers
 Association**
1742 Connecticut Avenue, N.W.
Washington, D.C. 20009

U.S. Department of Education
Public Information Division
Washington, D.C. 20208

Appendix B: Careers in Education

Preschool

Counselor
Dietician
School Nurse
School Social Worker
Supervisor
Teacher
Teacher Aide

Elementary School

Attendance Officer
Audiologist
Audiovisual Specialist
Bilingual Teacher
Building Inspector
Bus Driver
Cafeteria Worker
Child Development Specialist
Clerk
Counselor
Curriculum Specialist
Custodian
Dental Hygienist
Dietician
Groundskeeper
Home Instructor
Language Lab Aide
Librarian

Library Aide
Media Specialist
Nurse
Principal
Psychologist
Psychometrist
Reading Specialist
Secretary
Social Worker
Substitute Teacher
Superintendent
Teacher
Teacher Aide
Transportation Specialist

Secondary Education

Attendance Officer
Audiologist
Audiovisual Specialist
Bilingual Teacher
Building Inspector
Bus Driver
Cafeteria Worker
Clerk
Coach
Computer Programmer
Counselor
Curriculum Specialist
Custodian
Dental Hygienist
Dietician
Groundskeeper
Home Instructor
Language Lab Aide
Librarian
Library Aide
Media Specialist
Nurse
Principal